Horseplay

Books by Colette Inez

The Woman Who Loved Worms
Alive and Taking Names
Eight Minutes from the Sun
Family Life
Getting Under Way: New and Selected Poetry
Naming the Moons
For Reasons of Music
Clemency
Spinoza Doesn't Come Here Anymore
The Secret of M. Dulong (a memoir)
Horseplay

The Way Home: On the Poetry of Colette Inez
(Special edition from Word Press)

Horseplay

Colette Inez

Word Press

© 2011 by Colette Inez

Published by Word Press
P.O. Box 541106
Cincinnati, OH 45254-1106

Typeset in Garamond by WordTech Communications LLC, Cincinnati, OH

ISBN: 9781936370566
LCCN: 2011944442

Poetry Editor: Kevin Walzer
Business Editor: Lori Jareo

Visit us on the web at www.word-press.com

Saul, My Ally

Acknowledgements

"Horseplay" in *Western Humanities Review*; "Two-wheeler Spins" in *Pleiades* and on-line in *Poetry Daily*; "Little Pig of Beauty" in *The Great River Review*; "Attributes of Summer" in *New American Writing*; "Rooster South of Worcester" and "The Letter Before *A*" in *Barrow Street*; "The Maeterlinck Tankas" and "The Ravenous Woman" in *The Green Mountain Review;* "Private Hours" in *The Colorado Review*; "Galaxy Pantoum" in *Skidrow Penthouse*; "Letter From an Outpost" and "Journey From Santa Cruz" in *The New England Review*; "Not Mattering to the Earth" in *Southern Poetry* Review and on-line in *Verse Daily*; "In Etterbeek" and "Garland of Holy Roses" in *The Hudson Review*; "Vows of a Second Language" in *Parnassus: Poetry in Review*; "Belgium, Remembered" and "For Sarah Hannah" in *Big City Lit*; "Part Bull, Part Priest" in *The Asheville Poetry Review*; "At My Father's Grave I Remember T'ang Dynasty Calligraphies", "What the Air Takes Away", "Looking for Nana in Virginia" and "Reflections of the Lady Ch'ang" in *Ploughshares*; "Maroon Velvet" and "Ben Johnson Walking to Scotland" in *The Southern Review*; "Writing an Ijala in May" in *Chautauqua* and in *Chance of a Ghost*, Helicon Nine Press; "Crossroads" and "Crow Songs, Scotland" in *Hotel Amerika*; "The Spell of the Motherland" in *Quarter Past Eight*; "Any Woman, Ainu Woman, I Knew the Woman, Me" in *Monserrat*; "Reverie of Sappho" in *Subtropics Review*; "Children's Hospital, Hendaye, France" in *Salamander*; "Wichita Ruby" in *The Portland Review*; "Monologue of the Falconer's Wife" in *The Connecticut Review*, (Pushcart Prize winner); "Morning, the Couple" in *The Alaska Review*; "The Chairs" in *The Louisville Review*; "Marriage" in *Controlled Burn*; "Courtier's Lament" in *Nimrod*; "Letter From the Villa" in *The Chicago Review*; "Medway Sequences" in *The Carolina Quarterly*; "Horse Latitudes" in *Shenandoah*; "Pigalle" in

Rattapallax; "The Abduction" in *The Literary Review*; "The Insomniac" and "Butterfly Sanctuary Tankas, El Rosario, Mexico" in *Boulevard*; "Flightsong" in *Kalliope*; "Mothsong" in *Per Contra*; "A Chinese Workman Said" in *Open Places*; "California Father" in *New Ohio Review;* "To the Hornet That Wore Itself Out Trying to Escape a Screened-in Window" and "After Reading César Vallejo in New Hampshire" in *Artful Dodge*; "Witness to a Meadow in Virginia" in *Poets Wear Prada*; "Directions" in *Rattle*; "Hotel Magenta" in *Pot Pourri*; "Forest Sculpture" in *The New Criterion*; "Neutrinos" in *Confrontation* and in *Verse and Universe*, Milkweed Editions, Editor Kurt Brown; and "Quantum Mysteries" in *The Southern Poetry Review.*

I am especially grateful for the gift of time spent at Yaddo, the MacDowell Colony, the Virginia Center for the Creative Arts, the Medway Institute and Hawthornden Castle in Scotland, and to the New York Foundation for the Arts for a 2005 grant. Poets Philip Dacey, Charlotte Mandel, Wendy Ranan, Larry Rubin, and Pamela "Jody" Stewart provided encouragement and excellent editorial suggestions. I am in their debt.

Contents

1.
Horseplay 15
Two-wheeler Spins 17
Little Pig of Beauty 18
Attributes of Summer 19
Rooster South of Worcester 20
The Maeterlinck Tankas 21
Private Hours 23
Anagram of Colette Inez in a
　　Loosely Given Villanelle 25
The Letter Before A 26
Galaxy Pantoum 27
Letter from an Outpost 29
Not Mattering to the Earth 31

2.
In Etterbeek 35
Vows of a Second Language 36
Garland of Holy Roses 38
Belgium Remembered 39
Part Bull, Part Priest 40
California Father 41
At My Father's Grave I Remember
　　T'Ang Dynasty Calligraphies 42
Maroon Velvet 43
Writing an Ijala in May 44
Crossroads 45
The Spell of the Motherland 46
The Pen Man's Ship 48

Some Facts About Knute Rockne
   and My Father 49
What the Air Takes Away 50
Looking for Nana in Virginia 51

3.
The Ravenous Woman 55
Any Woman, Ainu Woman, I Knew
   the Woman, Me 56
Reflections of the Lady Ch'ang 58
For Sarah Hannah 59
Reverie of Sappho 60
Children's Hospital, Hendaye, France 61
Wichita Ruby 62
Monologue of the Falconer's Wife 63
Morning, the Couple 64
The Chairs 65
Marriage 66
Courtier's Lament 67
Letter from the Villa 68
Medway Sequences 71
Horse Latitudes 73
Pigalle 74
Love Poem on the Eve of a
   Foreign Invasion 76
The Abduction 77

4.
The Insomniac 81
Flightsong 83
Mothsong 84
A Chinese Workman Said 85
Meditations on 18th Century Song
   Dynasty Inscriptions 86

Butterfly Sanctuary Tankas, El Rosario, Mexico 87
Route One's Purgatory in New Jersey 88
To the Hornet That Wore Itself Out Trying
    to Escape a Screened-in Window 89
Witness to a Meadow in Virginia 90
Directions 91
Ben Jonson Walking to Scotland 93
Crow Songs, Scotland 95
Hotel Magenta 97
Journey from Santa Cruz 98
Forest Sculpture 99
After Reading César Vallejo in
    New Hampshire 100
Neutrinos 101
Quantum Mysteries 102

1.

Horseplay

Horselaugh from that hussy on the piebald.
Horsefly don't bother.
How many horses to carry the red

afternoon as it rides over the blue plateau?
The astronomer pins her wrists to the dust.
Hoarse voices. Brambles like stars.

Horsewhipped. Giddyap. Hearsay evidence
of horsehide, horsehair sofas,
horse heard naysaying.

She knees him where he's weak.
His hands on her shouldesr sweep down
to her breasts.

The hare's afeard of hearses, hisses.
Nightmares ride bareback.
Four Horsemen talking horse sense.

He says the universe hasn't run its course.
She races away. Mythical horses jumping light years.
The Square of Pegasus desires its hypotenuse.

"Here's looking at you and The Horsehead
Nebula," the publican nods to the astronomer.
"Ow, that's an 'orse of a different color."

The star bloke orders a White Horse Ale.
"Horseman, pass by, " the woman appears,
nice as you please, pokes him in the eye,

imagines the chap punching empty air
garlanded by stars.

Two-wheeler Spins

She wakes up and she's a bicycle.
Streamlined, at last.
Bicycles are naturally anorexic.

Sometimes her husband pats her seat.
Sex is not out of the question.
They're not a run-of-the-mill couple.

She wakes up and she's a rowboat,
sturdy in the water.
The couple she carries
are her parents, red-faced
and exhausted after sex.
She drifts in silence,
heavy with their regret.

Or she wakes up and she's a door
leaning against the bicycle
she once was, or a boat.
How to keep her husband
alert in these scenes?

He pulls out a key.
They're face to face
remembering excursions.
Inside their rooms, the parents
live quietly in picture frames.

Little Pig of Beauty

sets the swine style tone
in her pen. Too frail to breed, moon-hued lashes,
dainty trotters, all the rage through scented days
of corn, zucchini, beefsteak tomatoes
ripening in tune to her soprano squeal,
bass snuffle of the suitor
who overcomes her diffidence
until the blunt end of an axe
put the kibosh on her bliss.
At dinner I said thanks to a second helping.
From the kitchen mirror flashed back a twitch
of snout, eyes screwed in their sockets
blinking watery blue.

Attributes of Summer

Brown grow the rushes
you know hot hay
girl's roll downhill
and hard dirt thirsty
for cascades
a humble fall acoming
leaf peepers thwarted
it's the commonplace
of cracked earth
and desire
always forswearing
something or other
upon my oath
I asked my love
what he recants
at Lammastide
a let's pretend harvest
of shriveled corn
my rose-scented finger tips
the buttery shine of the sun

Rooster South of Worcester
(on joue le tennis)

No badass, Wallace without malice in madras
shirt and tennis racket, fault not

that damned insurance jock beneath the sun
as second man to your brash backhand.

Serve! Serve! Serve! Serve! You are impersonal.
Your couplets are you. I am as I scan.

Antaeus poet among pygmies. Serve!
Return! A pygmy forages for honey.

Forages and drums far from Cos Cob
and dreams not ample Stevens nor his lob.

The Maeterlinck Tankas

Not Maeterlinck's birds
sky blue flapping twitterers,
but blue birds at odds
lording over burnt forests,
scourge of crickets, moths and flies.

Maeterlinck heard their
calls high above the lilacs
each time he wintered in Grasse.
In *L'Intelligence des Fleurs*,
his *Philosphie de la*

Condition Humain,
he speaks of doubt in science.
Man does not belong
entirely to what he sees
and hears. A spirit life must

be built beyond our
sniffing through fragrant gardens.
Of Maeterlinck's bees,
those buzzing plump zealots, dazed
in the spiraling roses,

we may speak of a
subtle happiness, a blend
of mysticism,
occultism, and love
of nectar. When Maeterlinck

dined with the king—
it was nineteen thirty-two—

in my bassinet
I pounded on a pillow
and sought the everlasting.

Private Hours
(for H.E.)

Borges tells of a 15th Century fish taught to weave
in the Netherlands. She speaks an indistinct language
rarely understood.

Can the creature be a fish, for she knows how to weave,
or a woman who can live entirely under water?
Nothing was said of her vulva's briny taste.

We can't know whether she shuddered in the presence
of the priest as he poured wine for the Eucharist.

Mary Queen of Heaven in a sea-blue robe looked on
from a stained glass window.

A word about the priest.
At St. Scholastica, we saw his manhood through the
keyhole—a leg of mutton joined to a purplish sack.

Later we heard this well-endowed man was trotted about from
one lady of the evening to another in houses of ill repute.
What did he do with his gift or curse?

Did the crow devils snap it off?
In the riddle of the Sphinx what has four, two,
then three legs? Two legs of one lover, a three-legged

milking stool picked up at a flea market for a song,
four legs peeping out of bed covers, a photograph
of the Sphinx gazing on with insouciance, an indistinct

language of water mumbling along the docks.
And the fisherwoman—did she marry, at last?
Was she one of a two-backed beast on honeymoon

with little to say?
Sunsets in Cairo or Amsterdam blazed and spattered apart,
naked couples floated over balconies,

aerialists of love beyond a puzzle of countries,
Goethe opined that given the choice of quarter of an hour
of lust, no one would watch a fifteen-minute sunset.

Anagram of Colette Inez in
a Loosely Given Villanelle

I elect Leon not in nice zen zone
on lent zinc cot,
on lone lot I let Leon toil.

No coin. Toilet lice. Not Oz. On one
line, lone Lon Clinton. Ice cone. Eon on cot.
Tilt. I net Ezio. Not once. O note

oil on zinc cot, not niece, Liz,
teen tit. Tic. Zit. Not Noel,
Leon loin-clone, I let toil.

O colt, Colin, I lie on tile.
No nettle, lint. Eli on zinc cot.
I let elite Neil on line. Tie. O note

tone. Title: "Lenten nite on cot."
Once I let con Leo coil in lone lot.
I notice Lee. On zinc cot I toil.

O lit Lee, lent cot, I let none lilt in
Zen zone, not Toni in Olean, Leon, Leo, Len,
not Lena, Eliot, Eli, Clint, no Cleo on cot. O note.
I elect Zeno to toil. Olé.

The Letter Before A

waiting to be born
out of radio waves and ghosts of lost rhymes
unnamable as god in the void.

Carrying a presence dense with text,
the letter after *Z*, waits to be born

into nothingness—phantom dispatch of anonymous
names blown at the illiterate fair

attended by every invisible child doing nothing
and the little brown fox jumping and scrambling.

Aleph's ox horns, an *A* upside down,
and zed on a sled to oblivion.

Read me twigs blown in the dirt, veins
of porphyry, cranes in a line.

That alphabet of cracks on our lips, and in dust
lightly written, signaling hunger.

Lean flesh of words unspoken wait to unfold.
Meaning dances as we spin words, mysterious, reciprocal,

linked in marked conglomerations,
the alphabet of ashes in the absence before *A*

evolving to clouds
and the letter after *Z* buzzing with hypothesis.

Galaxy Pantoum,
(The galaxy Andromeda is speeding towards
our Milky Way and will collide with us
in three billion years)

Cows and people stare,
each on their side of the fence,
both aware of their differences.
Andromeda hurtles through space.

Each on their side of the fence,
sniffing clover and Queen Anne's Lace.
Andromeda hurtles through space,
due to collide with the Milky Way.

Sniffing clover and Queen Anne's Lace
children and cows stay unaware a galaxy
will collide with the Milky Way.
In three billion years solar worlds gone.

Children and cows stay unaware a galaxy
whizzes with light and dust.
In three billion years solar worlds gone,
all measurements rust.

Whizzing with light and dust
towards planets memorized in school,
where all measurements rust
in vanished archives of local stars,

Andromeda zooms towards planets learned in school,
past blackboards and boxes of space-age toys,
in vanished archives of local stars.
After class a girl nudges a poky boy,

past blackboards and boxes of space-age toys,
she urges him along.
After class that girl nudges a poky boy:
"At your rate it will take three billion years

to go home," she urges him along
to hurry back to cows in the field.
"At your rate it will take three billion years,"
she fusses and says "We've chores to do."

Hurrying back to cows in the field,
she prods the indolent boy,
says "We've chores to do
before dark and crows come home to roost."

She prods the indolent boy,
not judging the world might one day be
dark as crows come home to roost,
all cellular intelligence

not judging the world might be
void of crows, people and cows,
all cellular intelligence,
that nothing would stay as it was.

Letter from an Outpost

Monday

Dear Friend:
    What has prevented me from writing? This and that. Imagine the scene: a child watches its mother's convulsions and is taken ill when the mother gets well.

    A small but pesky infestation of borers leaving the corn crop bare. Roof repairs. We are learning the verb "to be" and conjugate all morning like a swarm of dislocated bees.

    Today Nando came upriver with a gift of threads, sulfa drugs and vitamins. He still wears a bone through his nose and looks a properly fierce retired warrior except when the Schumann LP goes on and then his face suddenly gives off a look of saintliness. "Music there?" He points to the player. "It's in the airwaves," I say, not understanding my answer but knowing it's the one to give.

    In the airwaves now a percussion of thunder and rain. Ahead of us lies a season of wet thatches and growling clouds. Why do I think of Clara Schumann fishing Robert out of the Rhine? Stalwart Brahms looking on. The children like goslings shooed away to sup on zwieback and milk in the nursery. I stray. If you were to abandon a piano here in the forest for a week, termites would eat every molecule of resounding wood.

    Tomorrow we start with long division. If you have two hundred fried grubs, how many can you give to five drummers at the feast? If there are one hundred band-aids and fifty people each with a cut after the games, how many band aids will not be used? Then there is the inevitable subtraction which reminds me, Makira's piglet has strayed from the hut. Dusty, toothless, obdurate crone, she insists on a gift to placate her loss. Meanwhile, a mate must be found for the sow scuffling in the bamboo grove.

    As for me, there is no time for anything but innocence and the burden of disdain, an outsider's belief that I will feed the worms a higher form of intelligence. I go to Port Moresby in the morning to take my body for repairs. The dreambook comes along. More when I get to the coast.

    Fortitude,
    I

Not Mattering to the Earth

On the day that we die,
    crayfish return
to their torpor, claws idled in the sand,
    bees dozing in the tattered rose.

Where frogs stop
    their perpetual wakefulness
on pond, bog, swamp,
    we may float in the scent of lilies and moss.

And in the sea whose sharks begin,
    at last, to drowse under shadowy reefs,
only to rise again,
    numbed by the cold,

we will join the angler fish,
    waving long filaments of dreams
that brush past our eyes, heavy
    with inconsequence.

2.

In Etterbeek

We reveled in our boldness
walking backwards through a Brussels garden,
past the potting shed, patches of furrowed grass,
onto a graveled path.
Spiders and bees intent on prayer
failed to note our passage.
It didn't matter to the sun if we stepped in reverse.
How we blathered to the waiting Sisters,
flecks of blood in their eyes that seemed
to examine our future in one glance.
And what we couldn't see—your place
everlastingly pulled away from the throb of roses
and their fractured leaves,
you, surrendered to fever, a soul flown
over the waterways in the province of Brabant.
Now slack mouths of old roses, what do they say?
I can't grasp that intelligence any more than I can hear
the thumbnail-shaped leaf as it spins messages on spider silk.
Hydrangeas transmute from cabbage green to mottled rust,
the color of dried blood from a pricked finger.

Vows of a Second Language

Conjugations of spoons in the refectory,
the prayers flavorless, root vegetables squatting
in gray rural outskirts,
the rich broth of Brussels a tram ride away.

These words like soldiers serve me when I call
for supplies, report on the taste
of that beetle whose back I cracked in half
and spat out. Bitter, *amere*. Listless soup.

And dimly remember sing-song Walloon;
our saints, on good terms with nails, hooks, blood,
the lacerated skin of martyrdom, lowered their eyes
or raised them heavenward, their souls reinstated

as mourning doves offering canticles
to orphans of contagion, earthquake, war.
In this picture, a child returns to the field
where her house broke apart, bangs a lost pot

to wake the ones who sired her.
Lêves-toi, maman, mon père. J'ai faim.
Around what's hollowed out, old smoke curls,
father's avowed cigarettes, his small vice,

the yellow-white descent of ash: *cendre, jaune, blanc,*
combed through mother's sparse hair,
all take wing towards the intricate city
where Charles, *mon frère en poesie,* unlatches a window.

In my fabricated Belgrade of his birth, light streams
through mullioned panes on which he writes
"night coming down, a dog with wings."
I, too, having taken the vows of a second language,

salute these words.

Garland of Holy Roses

If only my panties had been little white roses,
nuns would have loved my prickly pubis,

said be proud of your labias, doors
to the grotto of Santa Sexuala. God would be there.

If only my breasts had been lilacs, little scented
purple cones instead of fat pink mounds bursting

through my jumper. The Sisters would have loved
my damp bottom on a toilet seat, not pressing down

but blossoming like a magnolia smooth
and grand as a duchess. God would be there.

They said he was everywhere.
Nuns would have loved me. Queen of their garden,

I would confer with them, a mother Mary's lily groomed
for endless love of God, the infinite voyeur.

Belgium Remembered

In the beauty of the palms he was born.
Lord, he assembled,
in the purlieus of Brussels,
hands outstretched, eyes cast down
from chapel windows on rue
Chant-D'Oiseau in the province
of Brabant where I prayed with questions
I might ask the custodians,
their answers in lightning's
furious reply, and the frozen pipes
of the upper halls. There
we lined to breakfast.
Light splintered—
we knew nothing of refractions,
only apparitions, tricks
turning faucets hot/cold,
black/white segments of Sister's
robe, rose window panes bordered
in lead, his mother, Our Lady
dwelling in stone, that we knelt
under the spell of crepuscular air,
our rising Sanctus, Sanctus.
Then in that small country
edging the North Sea, I believed
when he called me
to the gate of his grace, and I rose.

Part Bull, Part Priest

My father threw off his holy robes
to ram the lovely cows,
Hera-like goddesses, though less vengeful.
When he left these *cocottes* in Pigalle
to their devices, he mounted my mother
near the Sorbonne,
her wet eyes glistening with awe
as she breathed a low moan.
The moon, a horn, rubbed
against their windows.
Seeds of milky residue carried
the promise of my hooves and snout.
Our galaxy, a thousand-eyed
cow, awake and vigilant,
even to that doubling,
and the one-backed beast
I would become
looking for my counterpart.

California Father

Sermons in a book embossed in gold,
a pocket watch monogrammed LGL,
these reside as my imagined artifacts,
and slide along the margins of his frame.

The reins he gripped as he urged
his horse to Our Lady of Wayside,
his riding crop and boots, let them enter
hours of clocks without hands,
time without flesh.

In uplands of California, earth tilts, sun drifts.
Once he came incognito, stripped of his collar,
to see me before I babbled words.
Now worn like a collar, a tightness

at my throat speaks to the restraints
he broke free of to make me
visible. He appears in me. From a filmed-over
mirror I catch the flicker of his face.

At My Father's Grave I Remember T'Ang Dynasty Calligraphies

Dispatched with a worn brush, the cursive writing
of poet Xaian Shu possessed heroic spirit.
His calligraphy's balanced characters
pointed to diligent study.

Scholar, poet, Mi Fu's idiosyncratic running characters
wrote of living in peaceful times before the Mongols
roared down from the north.

His writing was described as a "sailboat in a gust of wind"
or a "war horse charging into battle."

The long, slender strokes of Chu Suillang, T'ang master,
spoke of the donation of the body to birds and beasts.

Scholar-priest, my father signed his papers
in rounded letters slanted to the right,
suggesting an affable nature.

After the war, his bishop extolled in a letter,
"We delighted in his stories."
The dust of my father's body is donated to the mountains,
and wind brushes the name on his stone.

Maroon Velvet

In a maroon velvet dress, crisp lace collar and cuffs,
my neighbor licked pointy pink lips
when she asked "*Êtes vous Catholique?*"
I didn't say my mother language was losing ground
fast as my faith, that no confessional
heard my impure longings to be ogled
like a star profiled in *Silver Screen*.
Awake early, I slapped together what I owned
in the gray of a cluttered room.
The new girl's soft dresses aired on the line.

Sometimes I wanted them to envelop me
like the *Ave Maria*
she spun from her piano or *Clair de Lune* octaves
cresting like breakers on our penny stamp yards.
One afternoon, the radio blaring *Hi-Yo Silver*,
a moving van pulled up to the curb.
Stepping into a maroon car, she waved,
her scoured, rosy face not looking back,
the little pink fingernails in snug white gloves.
September, October, so quickly abandoned,
that empty house, immaculate, maroon and orange leaves
choking our gutter—a half-forgotten autumn swept away.

Writing an Ijala in May

In May I meet a Nigerian in the park.
He tells me the *ijala* belongs to the Yoruba,
that the word means to call out

with the sound of a conch—a blaring over dunes
to gather the villagers.
He tells me to write an *ijala*,

random proverbs are required:

> *The one who masters the puddle*
> *is subdued by the grandeur of the sea.*
>
> *Drowning voices pulled out of water*
> *live to sing of fish.*
>
> *To meet an elder on the path*
> *means one inherits a story.*

My ghost father swims out of a story.
From the depth of the ocean he has heard that conch.
Hauling rocks I arrange them for his hearth.

Early green attends the stones.
In May rabbits veer then bolt into snarls of plum.
The twisting course of the wind blows back the warblers.

Crossroads

Rabbit fur sky, the clouds gaining as you lose the view
of my mother's house by its river, the door ajar.
A snapshot shows her in jodhpurs and paisley neckerchief,
her back to mountains violently risen up—
unlike the valleys and plateaus I imagine
she and my father rode on dun-colored horses,
as if the hereafter of wings had been handed down.
Assume from her gaze she read his look,
arranged her hair for him on the pillow like a fan.
Another snapshot has her hair cropped short
across the forehead.
In one picture, his head's gone bald like an old Roman general.
The surprise of their child is packed off to the nuns.
What wasn't said fills this river house.
Before you turn back to the city, softly close the door.

The Spell of the Motherland

"O the mind, the mind has mountains..."*

My mother lectured the crow on the suppleness of song.
Like me the bird repeated what he chose to hear.
A damp wind from the Pyrenees conversed with her grave
 at Espiens. Half shapes, fox, goat, blue fish in the clouds.

No one said the beauty of the evening would shield me
from the facts. What remains will dream through
upheavals of earth.

"Cliffs of fall…"

I leafed through her papers. She wasn't as solitary as I once
believed. Postcards from the British Museum, Luxor,
Pompeii signed "Edwige," "Ursule", or by professors
excusing delays of manuscripts and checks. The long drive
curved into town.

At dusk purple martins annulled a swarm of gnats.
What hummed in them hums in me. Fire ants bequeathed
red welts. Overhead, red-eyed Aldebaran in Taurus
lowering his horns.

Here were the delicate veins of spring stars in the
province of her birth.

"Frightful, sheer…"

De la Tour, the custodian, sawed off a bough from the

plantain tree. I heard the river's voice slur like a woman
with a stroke.

How slowly she unwound her reveries in skeins of amber,
that eye color of my maternal side, Marthe, Marie and
Ambroisine—yellow glints in their irises. Medicine from
a brown bottle

trickled down my mother's throat. Papers that might connect
us nowhere to be found. His pictures and letters torn to
shreds and burned. Who finally knew her?

"No man fathomed..."

Wings closed, a Sulphur waited for the sun's decree on a
cloudy afternoon. I stepped through a swarm of my mother's
words: chalice, provost, gloss, internecine war. Lords of the
south marched with clanking armor through references
and further notes.

The day I left the house, a leaf spun down from that
royal palm planted by her father at the century's turn.
I heard the language of sweep and fall,
the shuddering disclosures.

---

* Gerard Manley Hopkins, *The Sonnets*

The Pen Man's Ship

docks under the sign of the cross.
Your thumb print on it, your signature,
curved, open, no intent to deceive.
I've signed on. Father, bring me the rounded family name
of your first school days—self-assured, a boy counted on
to climb on stage with the choir that sang Hosanna
New Year's Eve after the Great San Francisco earthquake.
And at your ordination to the Holy Roman Catholic Church.
I want to read those ink-soaked notes
concerning the councils of John the First,
indices and rubrics of that king's Cardinal, Langton.
Speak to me from a wave of papers, a fog of books.
When we sail, glyphs of clouds gather at a cemetery gate.
I dream we duck under the trees past your stone,
you steer into the gold flecks of my mother's gaze
at medieval scripts. A higher power of desire. I am born.
You receive the last rites before I first print my name.
You, my sire, giver of absolution.
Aboard your vessel, I ask for your hand in my hand.
You will never return wholly my father.

Some Facts About Knute Rockne and My Father

Knute's fame on the field of Notre Dame
and in a Kansas field—the doomed flight to L.A.
Rockne born in Norway, 1888, settled in Chicago.

San Francisco, 1886. First born son, my father entered
the religious life and took the Holy Orders.
Sent to Paris by his Bishop, he made a forward pass

at a pretty French historian. I hid in her proper tweeds.
Broken vows, shadows that stalked him.
He tipped back *le bon* scotch,

toasted Rockne, charismatic coach, convert to the church.
Rockne's plane fell in a field near the town of Bazaar.
Who was Knute in every corner of the country?

My father's body shipped from Paris to home,
the birth of a daughter offensive to Rome.
Notre Dame. He would have cheered its number of wins,

five undefeated seasons. Who was my father?
He gives no answer from a California field.

What the Air Takes Away

"Someone stole my name," a girl sobs,
 pigtails cinched with
blue rubber bands.
I want to name the bus
we wait for, *Huff*, the wind, *What?*
Inferno, sigh the fried potatoes
whose scent drifts in from a luncheonette.
Who stole the land where potatoes first were sown?
Who stole the vernacular of ancestors?
And that lost father?
I name him flute-wielder, a runner after
fire too-soon-gone-out.
I name him toad-filling-the-night-with-calls.
If I wept in the *Quechua* or *Tzotzil* tongues,
these metaphors might sing
to the goddess of names who offers
her shoulder to the child
that she may endure the departure
of her father's voice, inaudible as "*b*"
in *numb*, gone, invisibly gray like an empty bus
in a white glare of sky gathering snow
and the amaryllis lifts its throat to bees,
to cabbage butterflies and I slip into words,
what they mean when they come, at last,
to taste me with their tongues.

Looking for Nana in Virginia

She's in the purple cone flowers,
in the yarrow turning brown,
nodding to lemon lilies.
I hear her slighting a neighbor:
"She's flat as an ironing board."
Nana hands me an iron.
"Get your head out of those books,
they'll fill you up with words."
She's in my word pie, my alphabet soup.
The day she died broke the record
of a hundred degrees.
The sun a cooked squash,
her long-boned horny feet stuck out of the sheet.
I thought nothing was uglier than old,
crisscrossed skin, thin ridged lips.
Nana says nothing makes her sick
when I offer a kiss from this world to the next,
and the amaryllis lifts its throat to bees,
to cabbage butterflies and I slip into words,
what they mean when they come, at last,
to taste me with their tongues.

3.

The Ravenous Woman

Her dome of blue hair collapses into waves,
      delighting the plankton.
The Big Dipper licks at her hungry face.
      She devours rivers of fire and fire ants.
Bees sweep into her ear, owls glide down
      her throat. She hoots and hums
gobbling plateaus and peninsulas.
      Thunder wanders in her belly,
lightning jitters through her bones.
      She swallows whales for lunch,
prickly tongue lapping up tides.
      Famished once more she seizes The Man
in the Moon, spits out his bones,
      amuses herself with a handful of stars,
delicate as cracker dust.
      Not even a quake flinging her
a mountain chain from roots of the sea
      can dampen her unfathomable gluttony.

Any Woman, Ainu Woman, I Knew the Woman, Me

Ainu woman, blue lips tattooed
say she is ready to ward off
evil spirits. Marriage
may enter her in the shape of a man
with a headband and a large dream
of whales swimming to his spear.

Not that woman. I am no more her
than I am another woman warding off
fat-cheeked Baku, the eater of dreams
who squats on her pillow.
Marriage has entered me sweetly, flute music
in the forest. Orange minnows kiss
the corners of my mouth.

In her garden of millet and peas
Ainu woman counts deer and hunts them with a stick.
They leap high in her thought of them.
Only clouds fly more quickly in winter storms
on the island of Hokkaido.

The too red lips of a woman in middle age—
an odd mirror finds me on a city street.
Not that me counting clouds from a dune,
legs twined under a boy who stroked
the back of my neck.
Souls of unnamed deities drifted through the sky.

The Ainu woman overseeing her treasures:
cup holder, dog harness, stick, all inhabited by souls.

Death will tap at her window in the Time of the Bear.
She leaves in a ritual that reassures
her gods know her. She climbs a tree in a dream
where she drives back the bear with a stick.

I dream of leaving in the Time of the Fish
swimming out of trees on the island of Manhattan.
Fish woo me with tattooed orange lips.
"We are all inhabited by souls,
is that not so?" I ask. I do not drive them back.

One kisses my nipple and my hair. I am hesitant to leave.
It is time. I am a woman who knows a good thing.
My gods do not know me.

Reflections of the Lady Ch'ang

Half-awake she hears hooves at the door—
a stallion enters her Chamber of Longing.
When the door thunders shut

she recalls the fury of her childhood;
Mother's venomous beauty,
Father, adept at lighting amber

in the eye of the sexual god.
The listless husband picked out for her
has left her without heirs.

Beyond that gate the dreaming dog
paws at dragonflies that hover between heaven
and earth. The Lady

of the Hall of the Star that Rewards Long Life
conjures a horse to speed through clouds.
He balks at her command.

She twirls the gold charm sent by the lord
with his ode to a roan mare in autumn.
On tiles thinned by wind, rain, sun,

lie bare prints of her frenzied walk, back and forth.
Forest animals track the night sky.
The reconciliation she struggles to release

is a Leaf Wing pressed from a cocoon,
the cracking of the tortoise through its shell.

For Sarah Hannah

Daughters of Atlas, why didn't you fly
from your northern constellation
to pull her by the hair, honey-colored, long?

She required your strength.
She didn't mean it, she didn't mean to fall.

Hercules, son of Zeus, given this labor,
you would have grabbed her by the waist,
supple, flowing into a body

that contemplated astronomy.
She wanted to hear what stars tell clocks,

news from the shore of galaxies.
She didn't mean to disappear.

Sarah. *Sharah*, meaning princess in Hebrew,
we celebrate her intellect and beauty.

She meant to return to us, gold rings glistening
across that arc of the unknown where we look for her,
snared in radiance.

Reverie of Sappho

Sappho names pale stars for her daughter,
teaches her names for the running tides.

They hear the soft roar of the sea's lament,
songs of worn-down stones.

Daybreak lights a torch for the hours to come.
Sappho hums—bird phrases intertwine.

The curled wet lips of lovers, winged kisses
press against the present tense of desire.

Years will greet her with moonlight and grief,
her daughter exalting Aphrodite and Eros

in dance, body festooned with campion,
small, star-like white flowers.

Children's Hospital, Hendaye, France

One, two, button my eyes
so I won't see mother weeping.
Pretty Raoul needs a mother, go to him, I say.

Mama shakes like aspic
unlike our nurses in Hendaye
where I hoist myself between rails

and swim in noisy pools. Every day I drill:
you, left foot, up, down,
Mademoiselle Right-Leg, don't whine.

Mama complains: the vaccine came too late.
She eyes my cane and the gifts
from Istanbul, water colors, colored pens.

Draw me a basket at the wrist of a boy
playing jai-alai, yellow crayon sun
above his head. I'm their teacher, they obey.

Mama holds me fast to her scent of jasmine
and restorative teas. I paint a map for her,
red mountains, orange snow, green moon fingers

that rub the back of the Bay of Biscay.
She hands me photos, father, sister,
our cream-colored house.

She hands me plane tickets for home.
Okay, goodbye, hospital, I say. Step to the side,
I've come this far, get out of my way.

Wichita Ruby

Ruby goes to the gypsy to conjure
a steadfast time; regencies in Egyptian
cities of the dead: Pe, De, Heliopolis.
Under the Sign of the Lion, summer loses
to the carrier of scales who runs
with the Virgin and the Scorpion.

November. What are the terms of surrender?
she asks the conjurer. The cold has won
whatever wars the children devised
in the year, and Wichita Ruby, odalisque,
struts in her rayon kimono, a splash
of dragon at her back rising from a painted

sea, the ocean's little whorls in a reverie
of waves mounting the shore.
Another dynasty in the chalk beds of Kansas?
Another round of signs and men? Wounded leaves
sleep in the rain and over the hill a bugler's
song collides with a longing for armistice.

Monologue of the Falconer's Wife

As was my duty, I oversaw the carting in of birds
to taste in broths and cunning pies.
What does the falcon owe to the falconer?
Diversions, my lord, and uses for your hand and eye,

that you may watch blood spurt and confess
to the priest your love of the kill.
And I knew what the falconer owed to the falcon.
Jesses strapped to its leg, a leash, a solid block,

a covering to slip off just before flight.
Spoils of the kill, hearts of quail, pheasant necks.
These I have split with your kin and curs
slavering at tables piled with glistening meat and bones,

knowing you to plant your priapus in every arse
that sits at court, into sheep should they dance the quadrille
for you. Lord, I would sail home to my clan and sup on eels
and boiled cod. Send a falcon as solace for grief

at a barren daughter's return, and tell the priest
who prodded me to speak of our marriage bed,
say to him I am released from that vassalage.

Morning, the Couple

The man and woman sleep until the light
of late morning.
This is the hour when anything might occur:
a small fight over a real or imagined
toucan in their courtyard.
"A delusional pigeon," he says.
She turns the pages of the Sunday papers,
he repairs a broken shoelace, pays a bill,
reads an ad promoting a cure
for psoriasis which neither have.
"Not yet," he offers his sly
hypochondriacal smile.
They trust each other not to let things
get out of whack.
The super invites them to walk on his stilts.
They dance the tango under a sun
neither too hot nor too cool
to deeply bend their knees
or stiffen their spines in a waltz.
They dine on grilled nectarines,
syncopating towards an island of sleep,
above them transmissions of music
thrumming from a satellite
a thousand miles away.

The Chairs

Our faces caught in the mirror
above the piano soften,
hands resting on each other's shoulders
after we clear the dishes.
With a flourish you call
my attention to the four chairs
upholstered in my absence,
deep burnt sienna, color
of the wine we decant.
"this reminds me of…" you say,
lifting your glass.
Chairs accept our humble bodies
heavy with memory and longing.
Once we sat on stones
on an island in the north,
seeking the key
to Spinoza's infinitely
infinite universe.
Love, the hour grows short.
What was the comparison?

Marriage

"The thing turned towards you,"
is what Inuit say of reality.

Above the subway entrance,
a wheel of gulls

pulls the sky towards you.
The reality of my key in the lock.

Between leave-takings and volleys
of talk we remember

righting the boat we upended
that summer we met on the island.

The squeal of oars and your deep
voice in a replenishing tide

of opinions and facts rose towards me.
I heard fish sing our names

from the crest of a wave.
Celestial glory, hummed the fog

riddling geese and gallinules.
What was our trick?

Not to drown in the commotion,
not to give in to the calm.

Courtier's Lament

He's sick of pea-brained birds,
careless musicians on the branch,
of corpulent roses in dusty gowns
gossiping of former times
when things said were meant
to outlast the summer nightingales.
He's sick of them, too, drab insomniacs.
Yes, twitter, silly linnet, the hawk
is out of town and Rosalind's gone back
to the cretin who rules our affairs;
he'll have her head one of these damnable
days of celestial light. Darkness loops
its noose even for her who'll find a bed
under the rose, her briary tongue made tame
in the cold. And chancellor of days,
he'll not be the cretin's fool to pluck
all night, on a dulcimer, lays to the fitful
Rosalind, his strumpet, *tarantara*, bring on
the kettle drums, a crumb of music. Damned
small morsel this life proffers, nothing
will rhyme and the measure's askew.
Yet he will eat it whole that sweetness
near the bone of remembering two fools awry
when the rooster sang *cuckold thee do*
behind the back of a dreaming king.

Letter from the Villa

Crickets scrape their wings
in another summer narrative,
dig shallow burrows to feed
on leaves. You aren't here
to ask me for the time.

What time does the lacewing give
in its pearl-shaped cocoon?
I could ask the daisy
whose petals turn like the gears
of a clock, question the lizard
in a crevice of rock
the beetle dining on white flies—
but all of us are lulled
by the thrush's notes bubbling
from an empty court beyond the formal garden.

Squinting at the sky, I search
for your letters and the gardener looks
for rain. Nothing comes. The couriers
have flown to holiday spas.
What I see is a double set of wings
beating so fast they almost
disappear above the slender body,
brilliant as a fire opal or lapis lazuli.

Circling the pool the dragonfly
is a pilot looking for survivors
in a thicket of low shrubs. You aren't here
to ask me for the news. The papers come
late or not at all.

What can I say? That these bamboos
now rattling thin canes in the breeze
were a mandarin's gift to the Lombard Duke
Sfondrati, that ten carp in the water lily
pool doze in a reflection of blue spruce
pointed into narrow mountains, their summits
in the water? Listen, the bell tower sends
another hour out to fly. It dips and glides
as I set my watch.

Afternoon. An earthworm counts passages
with the measure of its flesh. You haven't
turned to me and asked: "What are those flowers
called?" Impatiens, and they edge the pool
where I study the wakes of delicate swimmers.
Do you know for all its darting forward
and back, front legs bent to seize the prey,
the water strider never gets far, rarely
flies though it has wings? In Lecco it's the same.
One thrust of the bullfrog's sticky tongue,
water strider and worms are one in the watery darkness.

Dusk. In a gruff monotone the frog rasps out
his old story as if repetition assured him
a place in the run of chroniclers peculiar
to the spot, a tangle of five-lobed ivy
and cushioned moss back of the villa's
water lily pool.

A spider's thin caul floats
on tufts of grass. I hear footfalls
on the steps, but it's only the gardener
lugging plumbagos to the shed.
What else? I suspect the common sulphur

now stopped dead in its track
has seen the ghost of Theodelinda, the Lombard's
ancient queen. Send word soon. I grow overwrought
like a goose unused to migrating the flyways alone.

The water lily is an ivory carving set
in jade. If you were at my side, I'd stir
the water to confuse the fish.
Meanwhile, below the perfumes of the villa
fishing poles cast shadows on the lake.
I send you a kiss fresh as snow from the tops
of these bare mountains, and listen for your voice
over the cricket scraps of song.

Medway Sequences
(Goose Creek, SC)

Green lizards skitter. Winter.
My letter wants to describe a serpentine wall,
the Landina berry red on a woodpecker's neck,

camellias in porcelain bowls, how grace
sometimes unnerves me.

Did I tell you the eagles' aerial courtship
was recorded in letters by early proprietors

eager to proclaim this low country
named for their king?

Our guide says one could be tricked on these waters.
Ten dog tags, a turtle, a brick counted
in an alligator's gut.

Now wood ducks vanish beyond the line
of yellow primroses used in healing melancholia.

My words on an envelope drop into a pouch.
Will you peer at the postmark and quip,
mail must come by oxcart to Goose Creek geese?

Am I the dubious goose flown in from the north,
lost in these fly lanes to my gander?

Jupiter has entered Gemini,
and Saturn in the Hyades outshines Aldebaran,
—silent rivals like the stone leopards

who guard this house, jaws tipped back
as if to devour frogs thrumming near the dock.

Horse Latitudes

Moon horses in the village by the sea,
a day on your book, talk of what wine
with lamb, fish, goat.
Sometimes I melted like a candle in your arms.
Sometimes I burned alone.

> At the ferry crossing, under white manes of clouds,
> I'd found your whitewashed house
> canting slightly to the south, a path
> of music to your door.
> You spoke of towns shut down at noon,
> others who'd left you for another sky
> deeper or paler blue than this gray.

Time cantered and pranced.
I looked for a constancy of light patterned on the rocks.
You looked for tonal counterpoint in the music of your work.

> Then the Year of the Horse stamped down, bareback,
> ready for our finding.
> "Come," you took me off guard,
> "before we squander our names
> like mayflies coupling at water's edge."

I gripped the tail of your white hair
and heard the neigh of waves.

Pigalle

In the doorway of a cheap hotel
we are a pair, hot and virginal,
your tongue in my ear.
"Get a room," *les cocottes*

heckle us.
In our embrace, I pass out,
crumple at your feet
A *petit mal,* you think, and plant

your glove in my mouth.
I gag, bite down and get up.
We are still there when I rouse
that memory from its sleep.

Fixed to the *grisailles* of winter,
before you leave for Africa,
shaped like a tongue on the map,
we keep failing to check into that hotel

and on and on until Pigalle
no longer pertains to Chevalier or Piaf;
the district rezoned.
Eons blink off the screen,

we swim in cloudy specks,
The Great African Rift thrusts upward
where lovers once moaned
through foothills of the Alps.

Continents drift.
Paris swallowed by water
and then the sun lashing the world
with tongues of flame.

Love Poem on the Eve of a Foreign Invasion

Natives flee on foot or ride
tumble-down buses to the interior.
From one year or another, civil disorder
looks the same to the golden plover
or to that stray goose roving over water.
Scratched on paper, folded, sealed, your promises.
Will you slip off her keys from your ring?
And the wallet-sized pictures?
Will they feed the hungry shore
shreds of her paper face?
War sinks out of sight only to rise elsewhere.
Through a sputter of distant fire,
smoke dispatches ghosts.
I will meet you on the bridge.

The Abduction

My soul has suffered
a misfortune.
My soul has been kidnapped
and taken to the Country
of the Dead.
Let the water-borne people
journey to the underworld
in a spirit canoe that I may wait
for the carver of my stone's
angel, dove, rose.

Death is never natural.
Sorcerers come,
enemies in the night.
In the dream hours,
canoes run aground.
My soul has lost its amulets,
owl claw, killdeer feather, bone.
The dead have carried them away
like a cough, or a fever
from the body of a child.

Mother of owls, water father,
sister who carves, brother who rows,
I will celebrate your prow's
hornbill, cockatoo, shark,
I will curse your sorcerers.
Release my soul
from the fog of the dead
to this house of flesh
sea spirits caressed
home at the water's edge.

4.

The Insomniac

Like a magpie she chatters hateful phrases,
worries this and that bone under a pool of stars
in The Swan, a smudged white nest at the Northern Cross.

Insomniac, she calls to clocks to deliver her another
day where ship horns appear to complain of departures,
and beckon her to release a list of grievances.

She imagines her skull as a bowl of pens scratching
real and imagined indignities on pages of the night.
A game. She must name a place and offer another

with its last letter. Altoona followed
by Andover, then Raleigh, Helena, Annapolis,
Salem, Missoula, Ames. She begins to play with sounds.

Selma, solemn, slalom, salami sliced thin,
thin in the crescent of the moon hungry
to be full. The insomniac appropriates the night

and imagines herself as a pencil in a box
opened by hands writing her failure to be more
than she seems.

Her detractors grow dense, a double cluster of stars
in Hercules. She names saints invoked by the wide awake.
Appollonia, against tooth aches; Dominic of Sora,

fever and snakes; Wolfgang, paralysis;
Thomas the Apostle for the Blind that she might have
visions of the Holy Mother drowsy in Nazareth.

The insomniac contrives Wise Men heavy with gold
under a wakeful star, smoothing a path to her furor
in the dark, bearing gifts of sleep.

Flightsong

Lovers in goggles and white scarves,
once we climbed to a glittering drift
where the images were clear
of The Hunter in the north,
The Lady in the Chair, a Swan, a Dog.
Now we start to disappear at the edge
of the land. Beneath us the runway
withdraws. When we take wing
I cover my eyes. Is this the gist
of the story that ends
when you wave to someone you don't see
and I don't see you wave?
After we plummet in a tailspin, who sees
us hobble away from the crash
isn't the point. We know light
won't go on splashing a path
for our takeoff and descent.
We are fliers in a vanishing effect,
crystal dust on icicles, snow on snow.

Mothsong

This is not the sun,
I say flailing my arm, but you believe
light's true source rules from the throne
of my 60-watt bulb.
I wave off the notion
that one day a hand will bang me to the floor
and I'll swear by my truth, one I conceive,
that or a lie I elect wholly to believe.

A Chinese Workman Said

the sun is a propeller,
great blades of gold
as I walk off the world.
My comparisons hold
in a blaze of untruths,
the government says.

Will I bloom again
in the engine's leap?
And the pilots, yes,
they testified.
Now I wear a numbskull's hat
and babble politics,
salt on my mat,
quarries of sky.

But my arm is a gold propeller.
Seven layers of industrious grief
speak in my sleeve
on the subject of flight.

Meditations on 18th Century Song Dynasty Inscriptions
(Metropolitan Museum of Art)

Chang Duo writes of a poetic appreciation:
...because of our natures we became close as brothers. Yet how can I match these orchids and bamboo or these elegant verses, their pure promise that we will be neighbors?

Prince Shen in his running script remarks:
...the bonds between winter friends, the fragrance of the like-minded have something which does not end in physical separation. So I inscribe these words...

How do I describe two girls
who burst into giggles on the other side
of the courtyard?
Next to a bamboo plant, dainty even in khakis and jeans,
they fiddle with digital cameras and chatter into phones.
My sisters, on our mysterious planet,
your century opens like an orchid.
Another spring scarcely remembers the silly airs
of my eighteenth year, stiletto heels, the ache
to write elegant verse.
Through the glass ceiling of the pavilion
purple-gray rain struggles with blue ghost clouds.
How can I hold the memory of these orchid-sky colors,
these bird-like voices?
Searching the fragrance of the like-minded,
so I inscribe these words.

Butterfly Sanctuary Tankas, El Rosario, Mexico

Released from the north,
Monarchs circle choked roads hewed
by loggers. Tourists
on foot— we say *papillon,*
farfalla, mariposa.

And ask the goddess,
Tlatzeotl for more fields
of stout-stemmed milkweed,
and appeal to Cotlicue for
long days of orange fire.

Route One's Purgatory in New Jersey

For the gain of heaven in the zip code of our area, we need
a miracle. Do the red-winged blackbirds that fly past
Rick Brothers Propane Gas, and Dinette Beautiful signal a change?
And the green anemic trees that sprout like acts of faith
on the side of the road, what do they say to us?

We who are crazed with delays pray to Bruno, patron saint
of the deranged. It is false to ask how long purgatory will
endure. Behind the wheel we must make room for angels,
vigilant to martyrdom and send up prayers while dolorous
rain mingles with sooty magnolias.

Industrial spring. Deliver us O Lord. We are stalled.
High tension lines transmit flows of power to dwellers in
suburban towns. And we, who abide in the city, to them we
cry, poor banished children of Eve, release us, to them
we send up our sighs.

To the Hornet That Wore Itself Out Trying to Escape a Screened-in Window

No shot at the Book of August
halfway read, hot hours,
cicadas plucking bass viols.
Off limits, the sky's
ultraviolet shutting down
in late afternoon to thistles
with their traffic of finch,
hummingbirds, zebra
and tiger swallowtails.
Out of mind, the Book of Grasses,
leaves, seeds floating on water.
I thought to release you
but feared your sting,
the pain recalled
larger than my notion of your loss.
Pall bearer, in my palms I carry
your body to the fields.
Who will feed on your carrion,
light as spider's silk
spun across the boxwood shrubs?

Witness to a Meadow in Virginia

Cows kneel in fields
fireflies have abandoned.
Soon another year of flickering,
a comet's shower of flowers in the grass.

I was born in another country,
Leopold, the cruel king.
I embroidered butterflies
on handkerchiefs
sold by the African missions.
A child, I said *papillon*,

and fluttered my wrists,
imagining shiny coins in boxes
shipped to the Congo
where children dreamed
severed hands of their ancestors
took wing on the path.

Today I bow to the swallowtails,
spangled fritillaries and sulphurs
as if they were royalty.

Directions

The river tumbles
downstream to the town
and the town thins out
to the sea.
How can you be lost?
The moon crouched
in the middle
of the day might throw you
off stride.
Take the long view.
Maps show depth
with deeper blue,
azure-tinted white
for the shallows
as you step
into the tide,
seeking that sheer green
wall of light
through a wave
prepared to throw you
back towards shore.
What can be awry
when the Evening Star
hands you
a copper-colored hour
on a jetty
built over sand?
Moss on the north side
of trees tells where
the Seven Sisters rise,
and using broad strokes,
The Lady in the Chair

prints her M or W
above the Square of Pegasus.
Look, every day
water persuades the earth
to recede.
Hear towns
chime sea chantey names in a line
hugging the coast,
to plot the course home.

Ben Jonson Walking to Scotland
(1618)

Jonson with numerous parcels,
porters and hangers-on set out
in summer from England to Scotland,
traveling the great North Road.
A hulk of a man, near three hundred pounds,
he scarcely slowed down through Islington,
Highgate, Finchley and Barnel,
Herfordshire, and Bedfordshire.
At Darlington he bought a pair of shoes
he counted on lasting the four hundred miles
where he shared a pint or more with pipers,
fiddlers, rushers, jugglers, puppet masters,
ape carriers, beggars, tinkers,
denizens of the road.

In autumn he strolled to court
to secure the praise of King James,
and took his ease in Edinborough
at taverns and inns.
Christmas week at Hawthornden Castle,
he supped with Lord Drummond,
the Petrarch of Scotland.
By the fire, they conversed
of poets and wits, Sidney and Shakespeare,
chronicles and treatises.
Drummond chose wine from a generous cellar,
but unlike his guest, made one glass
last the night.
When Jonson stumbled into morning,
wind hissed and crows contended in the glens,
past fields of oats and barley, dormant in winter.

Today neither poet would fathom the motorways
barring the old route to the Scottish border,
the metal boxes hurrying on wheels,
though both might lift a glass to cheer
the castle as writer's retreat,
where I read the laird dismissed "rare Ben"
as "uninformed and mistaken,"
and that Jonson's travel notes came to naught,
a casualty of the Great London Fire.

Crow Songs, Scotland

1.
The sun fiddles where the sycamore
confers shade, and were it December
of 1618, instead of this soft June,
Ben Jonson would have cleared his throat
to sing his tune in Hawthornden.
Crows' monotone, the concert
when he trekked from London
to visit Lord Drummond, both taking ease
from the laird's wine cellar.
Now their phantoms strum madrigals
or squabble over the merits of
Shakespeare and Sidney.

2.
A restless wind blows back the crows,
discordant composers. A melody of arrows
follows the king's order
to crush uprisings in the glen,
summons the gloom, rough voices
roosting in the tower.

3.
Milord Crow surveys his kingdom.
Well-met, he scoffs at devious cowbirds, cuckoos,
gargles *aargh,* sometimes encountering
his likeness in the window pane, battering
the glass with his beak: "Who rules here but me?"
Lord of the rook's dominion.
Nothing is lost in his grasp of the hour.
Dim light overtakes the crag, the ravine, riffs
of melodies twitter and twang their obeisance.

4.
Mossy underfoot, past alder and pine,
birch and yew, beyond that spot (it's told)
Miss Cunningham jumped, or was pushed down,
the nymph of the silvery Esk places a finger on her lips.
It's not known what the lady protested, her doubt
of Lord Drummond shouted high above the river
past crows wheeling above her.

Others say she was taken by fever
on her wedding day.
Lord Drummond, the Petrarch of Scotland,
waiting sixteen years
before he wed Elizabeth Logan,
said to resemble Miss Cunningham,
green cast to the eyes, golden hair.
Nine children dropped from her;
three survived to hear river voices
in a kingdom of crows claiming the castle glen.

Lord William Drummond, Scottish poet, 1585-1649.

Miss Cunningham of Barns, Lord Drummond's fiancée, was said to have died on her wedding day in 1616.

Hotel Magenta

Your hair a bear coat I wear
when you moan what is it from that
other time, what to do you huff in my ear.

Remains of a dream.
T-Rex on a cliff rears upward,
flames in the creature's eyes.

You wake to a neon magenta
haze of town lights through the blinds.
Between cool sheets I kiss

your scorched lips, tufts of singed fur.
We slip from our skins.
Bone on bones drums messages.

Fire flickers out. Lion. Whale. Snake.
Beasts wake the sky.

Journey from Santa Cruz

It's my story. I'll write it.
He circles my breasts with the flat
of his palm, calls my name,
the plosive "t's" of it,
his lips graze the back hairs
of my neck, smooth out lines
between my eyes, the mauve-amber shadows.

An envelope of dim light seals us.
We're delicate lovers and passengers
on a western ship becalmed, unanchored
for long days at sea, disinclined to return
to voices that claim us.

He says the voluptuous hand of his past
reaches out to him.
When the vessel puts into port,
on the dock a man he wants
blows a kiss that flies like a dove
with promises of land and risky undertakings.

Pressed against the rail of the ship,
I kiss the wet air as I sail away,
and they wave.

Forest Sculpture

Horns locked into blue air, head posed to tear
a patch of forest out of its repose,
this form was hurled down by Capricorn

to match a remembered self.
Earth reshaped what it saw—fire gods hardened
the surface to a dark shine, spirits of the woods

added their whim of tree stump and branch.
Butting faint starlight above the corridor
of trees, now Capricorn barely knows

its analogue whose glance seems to admonish us,
and like a divinity looks heavenward—
we turn our backs on the earth

that shaped us, the sky of our minds
lighting the forest.

After Reading César Vallejo in New Hampshire

Poet, I read you in the soft cusp
between June and early July
when I was born in the capital
of a low country, my mother
having crossed the border
in her last days
of cradling me in her womb.
Poet, your breath hovers over me
as hers dampened the pillow
on which she dreamed I was a bird
flown into her room.
Vallejo, that bird sings in this patch
of stubborn hawkweed
where I hold *coreopsis*, the word
for a daisy-like yellow flower
I cannot find in the meadow.
It blooms in the dictionary,
gold embossed letters
on a blue cloth cover,
that same deep blue of your poems,
and of the ocean giving birth to waves
in your childhood, and of night whooshing
above the train from Belgium to France,
easing my mother's burden,
the shame of me in her swollen flesh,
then a station called out
and doors opened in a line,
forever away
from holding her child.

Neutrinos

rush through the dribble of peach
at the baby's lips,
bowls of pabulum, raisins and milk

mixing with grit
from the split of beginnings.
Wraiths to our shadows,

they drift towards the teeter-totter
mounted in the yard.
Unseen, they'll propel

through that baby grown stooped,
quaint with her worm-brown spots
and wisps of hair.

They'll speed past as she tracks
powdery stipples in a telescope.
And lulled by dust

from the blaze of our star,
we'll have blinked away our names,
charged in a web

of spinning jots. You, me, them, it.

Quantum Mysteries

I believe in the offering wave sent to the future and past. The shiny black back of the beetle is there in both places with the bird pushed from the nest by its larger brother. When the absorber returns an echoing wave, reflected stars brush the fledgling's eye staring wildly at the rising dark fur of a mother raccoon. Hunger understands a quick meal. The mother dips her claws at the lip of the pond. Ecstasy waits. The needle-limbed loping mantis senses it and galaxies scrambling to the edge of the still to be known. Winds that scour our sun need not explain. Our knowledge lies in the direct path between what is emitted and what is absorbed. Your lips at the conjunction of my breasts. Isn't this all one needs to know about quantum transaction?

Colette Inez is the author of ten books of poetry, previously *Spinoza Doesn't Come Here Anymore* (Melville House Books) and *Clemency* (Carnegie Mellon University Press). The University of Wisconsin Press released her memoir *The Secret of M. Dulong* in 2005. Among her many honors are fellowships from the Guggenheim and Rockefeller Foundations, two awards from the National Endowment for the Arts, and two Pushcart Prizes. She long served on the faculty of Columbia University's writing program and also taught at Cornell, Bucknell and Colgate Universities.